Tot Lord and the Bone Caves

A visit was also made to Settle and to an unusually interesting institution there known as the Pig Yard Club. This club is a working-men's geological and archaeological society and has grown out of adult classes in geology started by Arthur Raistrick several years ago. To-day the club has its own museum which includes an excellent collection of minerals and crystals, and fossilised remains of one of those antediluvian hairy mammoths which we sometimes see in picture books and which apparently used to roam the North country in pre-historic days. The Pig Yard Club's visitors' book includes the names of Sir Arthur Keith and Mr Geoffrey Dawson (Editor of *The Times*).

Philip Radley, in The Friend, September 2, 1938.

Tot Lord
and the Bone Caves

_by_ **W.R.Mitchell**

CASTLEBERG
1999

For
EMILY SIMPSON

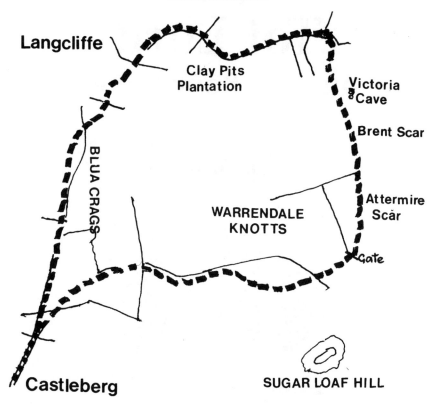

A **Castleberg** Book.
First published in the United Kingdom in 1999.
Text, © W R Mitchell 1999.
The moral right of the author has been asserted.
ISBN 1 871064 71 6

Typeset in Palatino, printed and bound in the United Kingdom by
Lamberts Print & Design, Station Road, Settle, North Yorkshire, BD24 9AA.

Published by Castleberg, 18 Yealand Avenue, Giggleswick, Settle,
North Yorkshire, BD24 0AY.

An Introduction

TOT LORD has been described as "an amateur archaeologist who continued a Settle tradition of 'bone cave hunting'." It began when Joseph Jackson, a Settle plumber, became (in the words of Tot's grandson, Tom) "the first cave archaeologist in the Yorkshire Dales."

In the springtime of 1837, Michael Horner, who was apprenticed to Jackson, was on the limestone scars above Langcliffe with two friends when they met a local man with two dogs. They were visiting "the foxholes," two small openings on a fan-shaped scree. A dog that entered one hole emerged from the other. Intrigued, the young men climbed the scree and, removing a large stone, made it possible for Michael Horner to crawl into a small cave.

Horner's spine would have prickled could he have known that he was the first person to enter the cave for 1,000 years – that in the spongy earth were bones and artefacts from a lost age. On a further visit to the cave, Horner picked up a bronze fibula, or brooch, which he showed to Joseph Jackson.

This remarkable man, who had an interest in science and is reputed to have taken the first photograph locally, obtained permission from the landowner to explore the cave. The entrance was almost filled with rubbish and overgrown with nettles. He was later to recall: "I was obliged to lie down at full length to get in."

Working in great secrecy, the excited Jackson removed bones, pieces of pottery, ornaments and coins. It sparked an interest in local bone caves. Others were found but none was so richly festooned with objects than the cave found by the fox-hunters and which Jackson christened Victoria Cave. They were to recall the life-style of the earliest human settlers and those who made use of the caves during the uneasy period that followed Roman rule.

Subsequent inquiry revealed much more. Beneath a deposit of clay, noted Jackson, "we generally find the rock covered with bones, all broken and presenting the appearance of having been gnawed." He had broken through to an inter-glacial age, about 120,000 years ago, when the cave may have been a hyena den and when what are now known as the Craven Uplands were the haunt of great beasts – elephant and rhino among them.

Jackson amassed a large collection of cave objects. He gave half his collection to the British Museum and half to Giggleswick School. Victoria Cave was a focal point for large-scale excavation in Victorian times. Then, in the inter-war years, Tot Lord came into his own as a cave-hunter. He was the undisputed leader of the Pig Yard Club that consisted of men who regularly met in one of the yards of Upper Settle. Their tiny room was to be described by Arthur Raistrick as a cal-hole [a gossiping place].

Tot Lord was no academic. He wrote little beyond the scribblings in his diaries. The memory of this amateur archaeologist and cave-hunter endures through the writings of others, through the odd file of yellowing newspaper cuttings about the Pig Yard Club activities – and in the memory of the oldest of the Settle folk, who still chuckle over his utterances and exploits.

My biographical sketch of Tot Lord is no more, no less, than a collection of memories gathered from those who knew him well. They included Chrissie, Tot's daughter, and Jim, who was his brother-in-law, both of whom have now gone to their reward, as the old Methodists would have said.

Tot's various activities should not be judged against the morality of our time. Archaeologists might sniff with disapproval at some of the methods used by him and his contemporaries. Tot, in turn, would have been amazed at the evolution of specialist aspects of archaeology and the glamorisation of it on television.

Tot worked when the mood took him. One of his great friends, E H Partridge, a distinguished headmaster of Giggleswick School, wrote of him: "His actual calling is a matter of no moment. It occupies the smallest part of his time and his attention. His sidelines are legion and speculation is the salt of his life. There are few things he will not buy, from heavy machinery to first editions, firearms to rare prints. His passion is archaeology in which his labours are prodigious and disinterested. But he is no cloister student, rather a man of action…"

As a dealer in this and that, Tot was no different from a host of entrepreneurs in our money-mad age. The idea of buying large historic houses to be demolished did not create much of a stir in the first half of this century when this was the fate of many hundreds on a countrywide basis.

My own association with Tot extended from 1949 until his death. Whenever I visited Settle on market day, Tot was in conversational mood. He was quick to follow- up a money-making lead, though he did decline when a collector asked him to filch a fragment of stained glass from a Dales church, remarking: "Well, I couldn't do that, could I?"

When J B Priestley and his wife, Jacquetta Hawkes visited my home at Settle – I was one of several contacts recommended to him when he was commissioned to write an article for an American magazine about the Dales – I suggested he might visit Tot's museum for some local "colour." Priestley agreed. Jacquetta decided instead to walk up to Victoria Cave.

I called on Tot to arrange a meeting. He said it was a pity Jacquetta was not intending to call. Tot had met her first husband through a mutual interest in archaeology. Later, at the museum, I was chatting with Harold Walker, a friend of Tot's, when I remarked: "To really understood these bones and artefacts, you have to get into the mind of Early Man." From across the museum came J B Priestley's fruity voice: "The main thing today is to get out of the mind of Early Man!"

Tot was his own man – a true character, well worthy of remembrance. The Lord family tradition of studying the dry bones and artefacts of local antiquity is continued by his grandson, Tom, from his home at Winskill, above Langcliffe. Forty years ago, in the Parish Hall at Austwick, I heard Tot Lord lecture on Victoria Cave. A short time ago, in the same building, Tom Lord gave an illustrated talk on the cave, its history and exploration. His thesis was that Victoria Cave was a Romano-British underground shrine used between the first and the fourth centuries AD.

Tot, born and reared within sight of Castleberg, at the edge of the biggest outcrop of limestone in Britain, had become obsessed with the "bone caves" in the 1920s. He was happiest when, at the start of yet another "dig," he began to coax from the debris of the ages the bones of beasts that roamed the Craven Uplands long years ago. In one of the inter-glacial periods, the district had sustained a range of fabulous beasts, including rhinoceros, hippopotamus, straight-tusked elephant and hyena. Some species are extinct. The close relatives of others now linger on the hot plains of Central Africa.

When Tot and his friends crawled or shuffled into caves, they came across evidence of Man in brittle bones and exquisite dragonesque brooches. They were following in the footsteps of those Victorian archaeologists who excavated a system that became widely known as Victoria Cave.

Tot in his Setting

IN MY MIND'S EYE, I can see him now, strolling across the market place at Settle, in North Ribblesdale. Tot Lord, greengrocer, dealer, wildfowler, local councillor and amateur archaeologist, looked every inch a countryman. Tot (short for Thomas) was fresh-faced and breezy. One of his friends, seeing him in fading light, wrote that his face "had the dull glow of old baked brick." He looked well even when he was poorly.

He loved to stroll about town with Peggy, his black spaniel, at heel. Tot wore tweeds, with plus-fours, patterned socks, leather brogues and a "pork-pie" hat. His jacket was invariably unfastened and fluttered in a breeze. In good weather, he might leave his jacket at home and go out and about in a well-worn green jumper. The stick that assisted Tot Lord in his jaunty progress across town had a stubber at one end and was used on his excursions on Malham Moor to probe mole-heaps for microliths.

Settle reverberated to the passage of steam-hauled trains – about ninety trains a day, operating on the Settle-Carlisle line which, in the 1870s, cut the town into two parts, with viaducts and embankments. Tot's interest in the railway began and ended with the collection of fruit and vegetables, consigned from the market at Bradford and soon to be hawked around town by the Lord family.

Settle market place sprang to full life on Tuesday, when market stalls sprouted like mushrooms in the space between greystone buildings, mostly of the 18th century and in the shadow of a Town Hall built to a style described as Jacobean Gothic. The Shambles, originally used by butchers, were now of multi-purpose. Shops were at two levels, with a terrace of houses on top.

Above all rose Castleberg, a limestone knoll edged by trees. Occasionally it cast pieces of rock. Mr Moffatt, the minister at Zion chapel, consulted an insurance company about cover in case the chapel was damaged by a truant boulder. The parson was gravely told: "If that happened, we would regard it as an Act of God."

Settle, a self-contained town, surrounded by miles of open country, was able to develop a life of its own. It was run by a Rural District Council that, based on the Town Hall, had the cares of an area the size of the Isle of Man. Needless to say, Tot Lord was a councillor. The arm of the law belonged to Sergeant Wright who, when provoked, lashed the offender with a flick of his cape. If the cape reached its mark, the victim was said to reach the other side of the market place before he stopped moving.

Tot was a man of two worlds – one sweet, one sour. A geological fault ran through the town. The sweetness was that of an enormous outcrop of limestone, lying to the north and east. The sour country, to the west, was millstone grit. Limestone offered him caves and gritstone sport, for at Settle the Ribble burst from a limestone dale into a broad and shallow valley where the river had innumerable ox-bows, looking like doodles on the map, and where at floodtime in winter the area was visited by vast flocks of waterfowl.

Tot shot for sport and for the pot. Once he bagged what he called a "white goose" but which looked suspiciously like a whooper swan. It was undoubtedly large. Long before it had been consumed, at meal after meal, the Lord family were heartily sick of the taste.

Whenever I chatted with Tot, our thoughts soon took wings and settled in the bone-caves of the scars. At his private museum, in the decrepit mini-mansion called Town Head, I was shown the skull of the great cave bear, which had been abundant throughout Europe during the Pleistocene ice ages.

Early Days

TOT LORD, a modern caveman, was born at Settle on Empire Day, in May, 1899, to a locally well-established family. His grandfather, Thomas (1836-1916), married a Miss Hartley, whose family kept the *Golden Lion* at Settle. Tot's father, "a grand chap" who had had the customary name of Thomas bestowed upon him, married Mary Ellen, a native of Langcliffe.

As a lad in workaday Settle, Tot was familiar with men going to work in the quarries and with women wearing clogs and shawls, moving clatteringly to their work in the cotton mills by the Ribble. A shawl was large enough to cover the head and might also be tucked under the arms, which was a boon in winter. The clogs beat an early morning tattoo on the flags each weekday. An operative had a can over one arm. It contained a little tea. She hoped to cadge enough hot water to "mash"it.

In summer, apart from collecting fruit and vegetables from the railway station and taking horse and laden cart on regular rounds in the town, Tot was cajoled into hayfield operations. His father rented a lile bit o' land near *The Falcon* so that he might have some winter fodder for the cart-horse. The Lord family shared a horse with the Parkers, who had a joinery business in Upper Settle.

Mr Lord, senior, was thankful when Thomas Marsden, who had some adjacent land, lent him a spare animal from the livery stable for the two-horse mowing machine. Marsden operated a horse-bus service to and from Giggleswick station and was able to turn out a team of black horses for funerals. When there was hay to be made, Tot was an unwilling helper. Jack Marsden, one of the Settlers who had migrated to East Lancashire, packed up his job in the mill and left his home at Nelson for several weeks, moving to Settle to help with the haymaking.

Tot's only sister, Cissie, married Jack Atkinson. They kept a shop at the top of Victoria Street. The shop had two departments – groceries at the front and haberdashery at the rear. Tot's father and Uncle Charles ran the family greengrocery business from premises at Warehouse Hill, beside "the cobbles," half way down Victoria Street.

Tot's childhood home, in Commercial Street, looked constricted but had three good bedrooms. In the same block of property was a cobbler's shop, belonging to Bert Young, who worked with his cobblers' last between his knees. When men, strapped for cash, could not afford to go to the pub in the evening, they used Bert's shop as a warm and inexpensive gossiping place.

Tot's interest in rural matters was acquired during outings with his father and with Old Nell, the family dog. The lad was already demonstrating his "magpie instinct." He collected and hoarded any small objects that took his fancy, storing them in cardboard boxes. Tot had an intense curiosity. When Tommy Earnshaw, his best friend at school, revealed that his father looked after the explosives store at a local quarry, Tot persuaded Tommy to join him in an experiment with the dangerous stuff.

They detonated it on open ground near Bond Lane. The explosion seemed to rock the nearest buildings and the townsfolk who rushed to investigate found Tot's cap lying on a still-smouldering patch. It was thought that he had blown himself to smithereens. In fact, the two lads, aware of the enormity of their crime, had taken refuge in some allotments and, when located, were soundly thrashed by their fathers. (Tot's mother tended to spoil him, invariably sparing the rod).

Tot went to Settle National School in the days when the headmaster was E E Roberts, known to the more daring scholars as Ted. He was a good teacher but could "lay it on" with the cane. The naughtiest children acquired nearly as many stripes as a Zebra. None of them resented such treatment. "I think we were better for it," said one. A contemporary of Tot, who was in the same class at School, recalled that their teacher was Miss Duncan, a dour Scot who, typical of the period, wore a black blouse and long black skirt.

In 1905, Tot surreptitiously showed the girl who sat beside him a penny during one of the lessons. When school was over, he gave her a halfpenny. This was promptly spent at Maggie Lord's sweet shop in Upper Settle. To children, Maggie's place was paradise. Part of the attraction was a parrot in a cage. If anyone went into the shop, the parrot would exclaim: "Packet of fags, Maggie. Shut the door! Shut the door!"

Tot left school at the age of thirteen. In 1914, aged fourteen, he collected his father's gun and ran away from home. It cost his mother a large sum of money to locate him and bring him back to Settle. Tot again left home and, at the age of 15, enlisted in the Army. He spent his 16th birthday on the Western Front in France.

Edgar Johnson, Tot's stepbrother, lost a leg in the Great War. The stump was fitted with a simple wooden leg which, when he was sweating on a hot summer's day, could be uncomfortable and was removed, to be sandpapered – a policy that could not last forever. John William Nelson, a quality shoe and boot-maker, found the luckless Edgar a job, training him to repair shoes. So, for many years, he worked in the upper room of a building behind the shoe-shop.

Tot was demobilised in March, 1919. To a lad who had experienced adventure and excitement as a despatch rider in France, a routine involving a horse and a cart laden with fruit and vegetables was not appealing. On the greengrocery rounds he was often missing, having lagged well behind to talk with a crony. (When, years later, the shop and warehouse were demolished to widen the street, Tot was to buy Jack Potter's greengrocers' shop in Cheapside).

Courtship and Marriage

WHEN TOT'S mind lightly turned to thoughts of love, he paid court to a distant relation, Margaret (Maggie) Lord, of Austwick. Maggie was a small, plain, home-loving country lass. At least, if they got married Tot would know where to find her. Her uncle, a hump-backed fellow, had the Lord family preoccupation with greengrocery and went on regular rounds of the Austwick district with horse and cart.

Maggie worked at Harden Bridge Hospital, half a mile from Austwick. On courting nights, Tot had to trudge from Settle over Buckhaw Brow to Austwick, where Maggie's home was invariably crowded, for she was one of eight children. (Three more had died in infancy).

Charles was noted for his leisuretime interest in propagating ferns. Uncle Bob Bolton, a sweet pea specialist in Essex also grew ferns and sent Charles a batch to plant in the chilly dampness at the back of his house at Town Head. Tot professed himself interested in ferns, and especially the rare holly fern, which was known to grow in the lime-stone grykes of Moughton Fell.

Those who did not know precisely where it was to be found might spend a lifetime looking for it in the grey desolation. Tot, who was always in a hurry, could not afford such a protracted search. He nagged Maggie's brother, Jim, who organised a family excursion to Moughton. One or two small specimens of holly fern were located.

When Maggie, wearied of searching, suggested they return to Austwick,. Tot was nowhere in sight. Then his stocky figure was seen on the skyline. As he approached, it was seen that he was holding a fern. He asked Jim, matter-of-factly: "Is this holly fern?" Indeed it was, being a specimen of grand proportions. A smiling Tot bore it back to the Lord's home at Town Head, where it was given space in the garden.

Maggie, wearied of Tot's advances, confessed that she did not want to see him again. When he came to the house one evening, Tot told a dithering Maggie: "I've got t'gun out there. If you don't go out with me, I'll shoot misself." His ploy worked. Maggie's mind was made up. They were duly married at Austwick Methodist Chapel.

There was no honeymoon, of course. Tot didn't hold with such things. He was not entirely suited to marriage, though he was genuinely fond of Maggie and the family. He and his bride settled in a cottage in Commercial Street, just across the road from his parents. It was a one-up, one-down place, with a kitchen added as though it were an afterthought. There was hardly room in which to swing the proverbial cat.

Buying and Selling

WHAT SHOULD TOT DO? His father did not intend to pay him a wage, "cos you'll never be there." He would provide him with the cottage and ensure that neither Tot nor his new wife would starve. The rest was up to Tot. Maggie bore him three children – Thomas, Chrissie and Margaret. And Tot, left to his own devices, turned to trading.

Grandfather was an auctioneer. Tot began to frequent the auction sales to buy cheap items, such as batches of books. The transactions never involved ready cash. Tot would remove his purchases, occasionally by horse and cart, and promise to return in a day or two and "settle up." The best books were sold to Frank Laycock, the Skipton antique dealer. Books of local interest were retained, being stored in a small building down t'Pig Yard, which belonged to the Lord family. The remainder of the books were taken to Roberts paper mill for pulping. When he had collected some money, Tot paid for his purchases.

A major source of income was from scrapping cars and collecting the solder, which had been copiously used in their production. Schoolboys like Tom Dugdale and Geoffrey Parker represented cheap labour. Tot would say: "If you come up to the yard, I'll give you a job." The scrapyard was a croft that lay between the Pig Yard and Tot's cottage.

The dismantling of a car began with the removal of the seats, the best of which were taken to the building known to Tot as his Clubroom. Tot next removed from a car its dynamo – if there was one – and items of brass, including headlamps, some of which were so old they were operated by acetylene. He put these bright and shiny objects on a shelf around the Clubroom to await a customer.

Jim Nelson, who knew Tot well enough to be able to visit the Pig Yard when he felt inclined, found the scrapyard a constant source of inexpensive items which could be adapted for camping. Jim and his friends had a permanent camp at Anley and the large bell-tent they maintained here was soon equipped with leather-upholstered seats taken from old cars. The soft "tops" of certain makes of cars could be adapted as groundsheets for the tent. When the Boy Scouts were formed, Jim's visits were more frequent. He would be down at the scrapyard, looking for useful items, when Tot would appear and ask: "What are you looking for?" Jim would reply: "I don't know until I see it."

Most of what remained of a car after "stripping" was heaped, soaked in old engine oil and fired. The blaze generated tremendous heat and when it had died down a heap of ash plus the solder remained. Tot, with his helpers, then filled an old oil drum with coke, put a bucket on top, threw the ash and solder into the bucket and waited for the ingredients to separate. The ash accumulated at the top. The solder was poured into bread tins and sold.

Tot, bored with repetitive work, and not a home-loving man, began to seek his pleasures out of doors, with shooting and angling. He ordered his life according to the seasons and was particularly active in winter, at dawn and dusk, when duck were flighting at the marshy areas of the valley below the town.

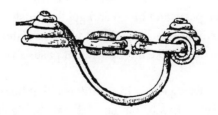

Life about Town

SETTLE, a small, somewhat isolated Yorkshire market town, had its Yorkshireness diluted by "off-comers." These included quarrymen from Derbyshire, child labour transported from Cornwall to work in the mills and, in the bustling 1870s, railway navvies building the Settle-Carlisle line who, when it was finished, settled down locally with their families.

Settle, existing in grand isolation from the nearest large centres of population, had a distinctive social life. "Characters" abounded. There were grandees like Walter Morrison, who arrived from London by train and, in good weather, might buy a side of ham at a grocer's, hoist it on to his shoulders and plod up the road to Malham Tarn House, which he called his "mountain home."

In town was Billy Slinger, the inventor of a curious motorised bike, and Arthur Horner, decorator, who was never known to finish one job before going to the next, leaving a trail of anguished customers. A local lady, fretful because Arthur had left the front room looking like a council tip, sent out her husband to find him. They met as Arthur was walking across the market place with a bucket of paste. Arthur beamed and said: "I was just coming to your house. But I'll want a brush. It's back at home. You take the paste and I'll go and get the brush." Off went hubby with the paste. Arthur, a bachelor, lived with his sister. Arriving home unexpectedly, he said: "Make me a bucket of paste. I've just let Knowles have the other one."

In the 1920s, Tot was gaining in confidence that he might survive on his wits. With Dickie Lamb, his special pal, he "gallivanted a bit." Neighbours were wrily amused when, returning to the marital home after a late night out, he removed his shoes in Victoria Square and covered the last few yards with the silent tread of stockinged feet. Tot did not want to awaken his parents, who lived just across the road. To people of their generation, anyone who was out of their bed after 9 p.m. was up to no good.

Tot and his cronies found no glamour in amateur operatics or in the reverential hush of a local church or chapel. He was fascinated when Bob Fell, an Austwick farmer, bought a Model T Ford and gave members of the Lord family rides around Ingleborough. The road surface was like a beck-bottom. When the driver saw some children playing on the road, he shouted: "Look out – there's another Tin Lizzie coming!" The children scattered.

Tot had no inclination to drive but enjoyed an occasional jaunt in the Three Peaks Country and would stare with curiosity and excitement at thundering waterfalls and a grey landscape pock-marked by caves and potholes. He entered a walking race that began and ended at Settle. The route lay through Stainforth, Austwick and Lawkland. Tot, who was podgy, determined to do well. When, during the race, someone offered him a drink of water, he protested, saying: "No, no. I mustn't lose time."

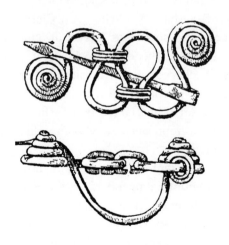

Picks and Shovels

SETTLE lies at the edge of limestone country, which is free-draining, with a short, floriferous grassland. Limestone rakes the sky with crags that gleam, bone-white, against blue-grey thunder clouds.

Tot's first experiences of the bone-caves were on excursions with fellow members of the Settle Naturalist and Antiquarian Society, which was founded on May 11, 1927.

Tot attended the inaugural meeting. Also present were Norman Thornber, whose family provided farmers with feeding stuffs for their livestock, and Dr Thomas Lovett, a proud Scot, medical practitioner, keen motor-cyclist and member of the Yorkshire Ramblers' Club. He rode his motor-bike to Gaping Gill to attend to an injured man. When out walking with friends, he lit a fire with sandwich paper, leaves and twigs, coaxing it into life by blowing down his stethoscope.

Settle had talent galore. Two professional men interested in antiquities were Thomas Brayshaw, a solicitor, and Charles William Buck, a medical practitioner. Brayshaw was forever at odds with the Vicar of Giggleswick, the eccentric Theodore Brocklehurst, and Buck's interest in local history was eclipsed only by musical matters, such as a collection of folk songs and his friendship with an up-and-coming musician called Edward Elgar. An industrial tycoon who had his name writ large on railway wagons was John Delaney, who imported coal and exported limestone on a grand scale.

Victoria Cave, a huge rent on the side of the limestone scars, was a Mecca for the cave-hunting members of the Settle Naturalist and Antiquarian Society. Joseph Jackson's archaeological digs between the 1830s and the 1860s had inspired them. It was Jackson who, in 1869, had formed the Settle Cave Exploration Committee, making it socially respectable by interesting local big-wigs such as James Farrer of Clapham, Walter Morrison and John Birkbeck. The Birkbeck family of bankers lived at a mini-mansion called Anley, to the south of the town.

Their interest in the bone-caves came to the attention of geologists such as Adam Sedgwick and John Phillips, also titled scientists like Sir Charles Lyell and Sir John Lubbock. When in 1870 a large-scale excavation of Victoria Cave began, the work was under the auspices of the British Association for the Advancement of Science. The project was supervised by Sir William Boyd Dawkins and R H Tiddeman, the last named being employed by the Geological Survey. He had been a member of the team who carried out the first detailed mapping in Yorkshire from about 1845 onwards.

The archaeologists transformed a rent in the crag into a yawning hole. Waste material from the cave was dumped outside, changing the contours. Among the bones recovered were those of animals living in a temperate phase of the Ice Age. (Subsequent research has dated some of them at 120,000 years).

Tot led a Meet of the Naturalist Society to Attermire Cave but arranged not to be present when Lovett, Thornber and T L Frankland, the Society's secretary, descended the main shaft of Gaping Gill as the guests of the Gritstone Club. Tot was not unduly athletic. He preferred to take part in the excavation of Lesser Kelco Cave in 1928 and 1929. By 1930, when the secretary of the Naturalists was Miss Adeline Montagu, a wealthy spinster who lived at Settle, the cave-hunters included James Simpson, a local cabinet maker and wood-carver. The work had the support of Dr J Wilfrid Jackson, curator of Manchester Museum.

Attermire Cave, long and sinuous, was reached through the negotiation of a scree, followed by a ledge. The system parted with objects from an astonishingly long period – from Bronze Age, through Iron Age and Roman times to Anglo-Saxon, as evidenced by the discovery of coins. A tremor of excitement went through the cave-hunters when traces of what was taken to be a Roman chariot came to light, among debris just outside the cave. The metal pieces were from chariot wheels, the wooden parts having long since rotted away.

Tot and his merry men attacked cave debris with pick and shovel. The days of delicate use of the trowel and brush had not yet dawned.

Emily Simpson, who with her husband attended some of Tot's digs at Kelco, recalls that in any case Tot did not do much digging. The methods were rough and ready. They suffered from impatience. Like magpies, they pounced on objects that glistened. They were thus following a local tradition, for the early Victorians had rifled the caves with the gusto of tomb-robbers in the Valley of the Kings in Egypt.

The Settle Naturalists, in an evening ramble over Giggleswick Scar, visited Kinsey Cave, which had been worked for many years by W Kinsey Mattinson, of Austwick, and was named after one of his Christian names. A local newspaper noted that "many relics of the Celtic and Romano-British period are to be gleaned from the limestone hills around Settle," and that shortly a burial barrow above Castleberg at Settle was to be opened.

When Tot and his men were excavating in Attermire Cave, on a scar overlooking Stockdale, Jackson's help with identification and chronology was invaluable. Jackson had excavated in various parts of the world, building up a reputation for his ability to identify the bones of long-dead birds and beasts, even tiny creatures, such as vole, shrew and lemming. A special technique he adopted with the latter was to fill a biscuit tin with cave-clay and take it home, placing it in the oven overnight and then breaking up the dried clay, in which the small bones were clearly delineated. Even when he went blind, Jackson was able to identify bones by touch and texture.

It was a wet period. Jackson reported "much drip in the cave" and noted that "on several occasions the cave diggers were wet through in a very short space of time. The wet and sticky condition of the cave-earth also hampered the work as the material had to be brought out to the entrance and worked through by the hand."

Attermire had already been rifled, and from it had been brought Roman coins and the skeleton of an adult human. Now, in 1930, the finds included bronze dragonesqe-type fibulae, spindle whorls made of bone or stone, a weaving-comb made of deer antler, and lots of animal bones, of both domesticated and wild stock. Inevitably, among such a temperamental group of cave-hunters, there were differences of opinion. Jackson, "set up" by the others, quit the work and took with him all the information he had gathered about life in the Craven caves.

Tot's fascination with the caves was further stimulated by a series of lectures given locally by Dr Arthur Raistrick, of Armstrong College, Newcastle. They needed each other. Raistrick, a Quaker, who lived an austere life, benefited from Tot's considerable archive of material he had picked up here and there. Tot liked to associate himself with people he might secretly think of as his "betters." Eventually, Tot and his cronies were spending up to 50 Sundays a year "up by Victoria Cave." They could forget the cares of a workday world as they pieced together evidence of life thousands of years ago.

Tot got his priorities right, making a fire, on which he placed a pan of water. When the water began to bubble he would add "carrots, turnips and other vegetables he had got out of his shop." The outcome was a stew, meeting the demands of the "inner man." For it was said in Yorkshire: "It's thi stomack 'as 'ods thi back up." Tot, camping on Malham Moor, during a dig, had a tent large enough to hold a bed, table and chairs.

Bill Hill, of Colne, was fond of relating a story about how Tot, Jim Haygarth and another man decided they would explore Victoria Cave to the end, which was much further than the spacious cave seen by most visitors. As the trio crawled further into the hillside, they encountered a very low and narrow section. Jim, who was leading, and the other man, managed to squeeze through this section but Tot became wedged tight in the horizontal passage, much to the amusement of his friends.

As Tot struggled to retreat with a satchel full of rock specimens, this worked up his body until he could move neither backwards or forwards. Jim said: "What the hell are we laughing for? We're on the wrong side!" They freed Tot by cutting and tearing his jacket. Then Jim lay flat on his back and with his feet on Tot's shoulders pushed Tot out of the narrow section "like a cork out of a bottle."

The limestone country held intriguing bumps – the burial places of ancient people – and everywhere were the remains of ancient settlements, but Tot's initial concern was to clean out the caves, with

Attermire receiving early attention. When it was too narrow to go any further, he enlisted a band of helpers to widen the passage. This being considered too slow, they began to use explosives.

Tot and his cronies equipped themselves with spades, trowels, acetylene lamps and ropes. At Kelco Cave, near Giggleswick Quarry, cave material was hauled into the open by rope and bucket, to be sieved for the removal of interesting artefacts. They took food for t'day, and returned with "bits o' bones."

Work in Victoria Cave, which was supposed to have been exhausted by Mr Tiddeman and others in the 1870s, yielded yet another ancient treasure - a weapon, found in a deposit of cave-earth previously overlooked. Tot described the object as a point of reindeer horn, about nine inches long, sharpened at one end and bevelled off with a flat side at the other, evidently that it might be attached to a wooden shaft.

In the Pig Yard

THE CELEBRATED Pig Yard Club (prop: Tot Lord) came into being when Tot began using a tiny room down his father's yard in Upper Settle as a dumping place for odds and ends he might one day be able to sell. There were several such yards in a part of town where a green – albeit, a sloping green – gives the impression of a separate village. Old cottages, outbuildings, and a Victorian terrace, cluster together as though afraid of slipping.

We have no precise date for the formation of the Pig Yard Club. Like Topsy, it just growed. No minute book was kept. The so-called clubroom was simply a cal-oil, a place for chattering about this and that, as was the cobbler's shop in an earlier period. The Pig Yard, a place where pigs were slaughtered, also held the stable for the horse. There was a well at which the horse might drink. Hay made at rented meadows was transported by horse-drawn cart to be stored down the yard. Local gardeners disposed of the horse dung.

The door of the Pig Yard Clubroom was split into two, as on a stable door. Inside the building was a table and, around the walls, sprung-seats from scrapped cars. Lengths of shelving held the most saleable of items stripped from cars, including dynamos, brass headlamps and horns that blared when someone squeezed a rubber bulb. Between the Pig Yard Club and the road was a building used by the Council as a store for such items as spades and also a wooden snow plough which, when in action, was drawn by horses.

The Pig Yard Club had no officials. "The members mucked in." Naturally, Tot's ideas prevailed. Arthur Raistrick recalled that the diminutive meeting place was heated by a coke stove. The Pig Yarders were a varied lot. Alf Sewell, tall and thin, had a fund of the latest gossip, being a hairdresser employed by John Hunt at one of the shops fringing the bottom storey of the Town Hall. Alf, who lived with his sisters at Giggleswick, achieved a measure of immortality when his surname was given to a newly-excavated system just north of Giggleswick Scar. This was henceforth referred to as Sewell's Cave.

Regulars at the Pig Yard get-togethers were John Dinsdale, road foreman, and Billy Shuttleworth, a farmer. Three members of the Breaks family were among Tot's close friends. Robert helped him to break up old cars. Thomas Breaks, a solicitor's clerk, and Billy Breaks, undermanager at t'Quarp (officially the Co-operative stores) lent their special skills to the task of cave exploration. William Thomas Briggs, one of the

COAT OF ARMS OF THE PIG YARD CLUB

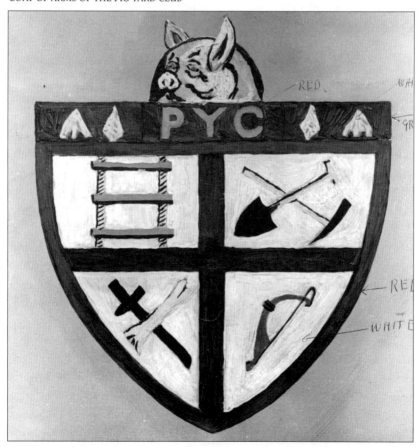

founders of the PYC, dealt with social matters, including an annual fishing trip to Greenodd, where the Leven flows into Morecambe Bay.

Albert Mitchell gave press coverage to the Club's successes. Tot and his fellows frequently featured in notes written for the *Craven Herald & Pioneer*. At one stage, the Pig Yard appeared as the Settle Cave Club, "a party of amateur archaeologists whose membership is recruited from Settle, Giggleswick, Langcliffe, Gargrave and Skipton." In September, 1935, they had discovered "yet another link with the British-Romano period in the Craven district…"

Tot, described as the founder of the Club, was "an experienced antiquary who for many years now has been excavating cave dwellings and early British encampments in an area bounded on the one hand by Giggleswick Scars and on the other by Malham Tarn." Albert reported that "Jubilee Chamber [in King's Scar, above Langcliffe], where the skeletons were found…had to be excavated in stooping posture by the light of a high-powered lamp. Meals, also, were cooked in this cavern, and until a more convenient entrance was made recently, it was no uncommon experience for the members of the Club to spend several hours underground."

Tot seemed to be able to smell out antiquities. He just happened to be present on marshy ground near the Ribble at Long Preston in April, 1933 when men who were digging a hole for one of the standards of a electric cable came across the horns and skull of a giant, prehistoric ox. Tot knew the Ribble Valley as well as any man. In his spare time, in winter, he would collect his gun and saunter to the riverside to await the evening flight of duck. Often he had the company of E H Partridge, the distinguished headmaster of Giggleswick School.

He told Partridge there were some wild geese on the river at Runley Bridge. Would he like to have a go at them? When the subject of trespass was raised, Tot said he had permission to shoot there.

They had slain a couple of geese when the water bailiff appeared to view. Tot's manner change. Excitedly, he said to Partridge: "You'll have to run for it now!" They scrambled across the river and reached the sanctuary of Giggleswick School by a long and devious route.

Enter Eli Simpson

UNTIL THE 1930s, the exploration of the limestone underworld was regarded as a sporting-science. During this period, the three best-known Settle cavers were Tot Lord, Eli Simpson and Norman Thornber. Eli emphasised the scientific aspect and built up an impressive archive of caving discoveries. In 1932, he joined the Craven Pothole Club but soon resigned. He and Tot Lord were incompatible, being "friends who fell out with each other fairly often."

Eli, when signing personal letters and notes, invariably spelt his nickname Cymmie. His involvement with the official side of caving had begun when he was the driving force behind the Yorkshire Speleological Association, which he founded with Frederic Haworth. The first meet took place at the Hill Inn, Chapel-le-Dale, in April, 1906. In 1932, Cymmie became "Cave Secretary" of the Settle Naturalist and Antiquarian Society. Thereafter he caved more or less independently of the clubs, often with Peter B Binns and Peter Longbottom.

Tot had the virtue of being a "local." Cymmie was classifiable as "off-comer," being a native of the Leeds area. For a time he lived in Austwick. Then, in July, 1935, when the need for a co-ordinating body for the many individuals, groups and clubs engaged in caving was met by the British Speleological Association, the headquarters for the first three years were at Cragdale, Settle.

Tot was involved in a proposal (when it was known only to a few, though presumably to Cymmie) to make Settle the permanent home of the British Speleological Association. Monica, the daughter of local historian Dr C W Buck and now married to Orlando Greenwood, referred to "that delicate affair" in a letter to Tot written from her home in Richmond, Surrey. Mrs Marlor (Monica's mother-in-law by her first marriage) was seeking to arrange a meeting between Lady Boyd Dawkins, Sir Arthur Keith and Miss C Delaney, the wealthy daughter of

John Delaney. At such a meeting the subject would be broached. Settle would be an ideal headquarters for speleological activity. (The Wills family were keen to see such a caving centre based on Bristol).

Financial help would be needed to acquire suitable premises, those mentioned by Monica being Cragdale, in Duke Street, and the Folly. "Do not confide this letter, or any mention of it, to your most intimate acquaintance," added Monica. The move was made to Cragdale, the property being rented, not owned. Eli Simpson was the man who made his home and office at this splendid building in Duke Street. The first issue of *Caves and Caving* (June, 1937) carried an attractive picture by E Simpson of Cragdale seen across a spacious well-kept lawn and captioned "The New Headquarters."

This picture is on the inner front cover. The text beneath the picture says: "It is intended that Cragdale shall be at once a co-ordinating centre for the work of the Association and a national museum of anthropological, archaeological, geological and prehistoric matter relating to caves and potholes. The extensive grounds will offer scope for the display of open-air exhibits and for other developments."

The BSA leased most of the building, and catering facilities were at hand through a quite separate enterprise, The Curlew Café. There was consternation when a flock of sheep being driven from Settle railway station to Stockdale went off course and invaded the café through its French windows. Eventually, Cymmie moved – with his copious files – to Commercial Yard. The building became stuffed with books and caving records.

Here, too, were cave photographs, reproduced at enormous size, a feat made possible when Cymmie cut a hole in the top floor of the building and projected the beam of light through the hole on to sensitive paper placed on the floor below. He photographed the main chamber of Gaping Gill using a plate camera and flash powder. The powder was strewn on crumpled sheets of newspaper placed in various parts of the chamber. Cymmie, having taken a lens hood from the camera, ignited the flashpowder in stages. Smoke filled the vast chamber. He was left with the difficult task of locating the camera in the man-made fog.

Cymmie, a man of fiery temperament and autocratic manner, wanted Things to be done *his* way. "Even though he maintained an air of courtesy, and kept in touch with the others, there was little or no cooperation beneath his veneer of harmony" writes a caving historian. An emergency special general meeting of the BSA was held at Leicester on October 15, 1938, to consider the financial position of the Association. The meeting discussed either raising subscriptions or cutting down expenditure by relinquishing Cragdale at Settle. Tot complained that many northern BSA members, including himself, had been refused admission to the records at Cragdale, a claim which Cymmie denied.

The disagreement appears to have arisen over an old map of Ingleton which Cymmie had acquired. Tot wanted this for this museum. Indeed, there were now four rival museums at Settle – those of the BSA, the Pig Yard Club, the Settle Naturalist and Antiquarian Society and Giggleswick School. Tot, who ran the Pig Yard Club, was an active member of the BSA and also of the affiliated Settle Naturalists. And, to add to the administrative confusion, Giggleswick School was the venue of the BSA annual conference in 1938.

During the uneasy relationship between Cymmie and Tot, each was continually on guard in case the other secured an advantage. Yet the two men complimented and needed each other. Tot's genius was in stumbling over, buying or begging documents and artefacts which proved to be important in Cymmie's ceaseless researches.

A prime example was that of some of the Ribblesdale Papers, reports by Lord Ribblesdale's agent at Malham Tarn concerning the calamine mine at Pikedaw in Grizedale, between Settle and Malham, and also the Fountains Fell colliery. These papers were among the items on sale when the estate was wound up. His wealthy brewer friend, Bradfer-Lawrence, loaned them to Tot, who in turned passed them to Cymmie. He typed them out attractively and copied a plan of the calamine mine. (Arthur Raistrick also had access to the documents via Tot. He used this prime source material without acknowledgement to Tot and meanwhile wrote to Tot of his constant admiration for him in rescuing such material).

Tot, having fed Cymmie with such useful source material about mining for calamine at Pikedaw, was naturally annoyed when he heard that some young members of the BSA had been persuaded to visit the Pikedaw caverns without telling him. In Tot's view, this was devious. The friendship between the two men soured once again. Cymmie mollified Tot by taking him down Pikedaw and showing him around.

After this period of coolness, they made up their friendship and continued to trade things off to each other. Cymmie, sitting in his office, was heard by some cavers to make unkind remarks about Tot as Tot arrived to see him. Cymmie, sweet and charming, immediately said: "Come in, Tot, my old friend."

In the end, it was Tot, the extrovert, who would be remembered most vividly. Cymmie, the off-comer, and an introvert, was an office type. He used his time constructively, building up the archive. Cymmie did play some nasty tricks in pursuit of archive material. He claimed the books and pamphlets of the Settle Recording Society that had been housed at its headquarters in the Assembly Rooms but were now being disposed of because the Society could not afford to pay the rent. Cymmie grabbed all the material, including old Brayshaw scrapbooks that were on loan from the Lambert family. The family got them back, having produced the receipt from the Recording Society, but before returning them, Cymmie coolly "plucked" from them a host of old photographs.

At the third annual conference of the British Speleological Association at Giggleswick School in 1938, Tot addressed the delegates, uttering some good, popular, reportable stuff. In one of few recorded observations on his work in the bone-caves, Tot remarked that his discoveries had led him to conclude that cave-dwellers spent much of their time at the entrances of their uncomfortable homes.

This theory had been confirmed by finding fragments of cooking pots and the discovery of large fire hearths and various implements and utensils. "I find it difficult to explain, however, why early man lived in these caves. In the Jubilee Cave there was headroom of only three feet and in Victoria Cave of four feet. The caves would be damp, dark places, and a good shower of rain would percolate through the shallow roof."

He concluded, "judging by signs of habitation in adjoining fields, that cave-dwellers probably spent the entire summer out of doors, resorting to the caves only in severe winters and at times of threatened attack." Dr Jackson got his chronology wrong when told the Conference of his belief that the lives of these primitive families must have been full of excitement. There abounded in the region of the caves such animal companions as the hippopotamus, the long-tusked elephant and a now extinct species of rhinoceros. (Man was hardly contemporary with these beasts). There were also hyenas, bears, reindeer and lynx. "At the time the peaceful River Ribble was the favourite drinking ground for families of elephants, the prey of lions and hyenas."

*Photographs
from the
Lord family
collection*

*Above:
Tot as many will
remember him.*

*Right:
In his beloved
limestone
country.*

Above: In the Pig Yard, Upper Settle. *Below:* Army service in the 1914-18 war (Tot is second from the left of those standing).

*Snapshots
from
Feizor*

Photograph: Yorkshire Observer

Wapping Hall, the redundant Primitive Methodist chapel in Upper Settle, when Tot had converted it into his Pig Yard Club museum. Tot is with his son, Thomas. Note the candelabra and the shield on the wall (for details see page 26).

Photograph: W R Mitchell

Antiques Under Glass

Tot stands before the skull of the great cave bear when the Museum had been transferred to Town Head, Settle. He ensured that each of his exhibits – even a stuffed badger – was behind glass. The great cave bear's skull was recovered from Victoria Cave. A visitor to the museum later wrote: "On the basis of an elementary education in the local school – and a love of natural history inherited from his father –Tot has built up a tremendous store of knowledge."

My dear Tot Lord.

It gives me great pleasure to write my name in your book. You have been a great pioneer in what you have done for the "Prehistorics" of Settle. We are all your debtors. With my best wishes for the success of all your plans. I am

Yours of olden times

Arthur Keith .

Downe. Kent.
May 17 1950

Inscription by Sir Arthur Keith on the flyleaf of his autobiography. Tot, as a young man, had sent the great scientist bones for examination. Sir Arthur wrote: "I know professional archaeologists scowl on Tot Lords. I have a love for them…"

Above: Tot, with Mr and Mrs Arthur Simpson at Lowther Castle on one of the days the contents were being sold.
Below: Tot with the long-chassis Land Rover bought for him by Arthur Simpson, of Gargrave.

HLBL/JWC.

Sharow End,
Ripon, Yorks.

3rd May, 1954.

Tot Lord, Esq.,
Townhead,
Settle, Yorks.

My dear Tot,

     I got the cauldron to the British Museum
safely last week. My friend, Sir Thomas Kendrick,
the Director, asked me if this was found in the
same place as the brooch which they have. I
think that is so, but can you mark on a local
ordnance sheet the exact spot where it was found,
and what other objects were found in association
with it? Or would you rather I asked Mr. W.
Mattinson?

     You need not bother to reply to this, but
have it all ready for me on Saturday, when I
hope we shall meet with the Alpine Garden lot.

     With kind regards,

Yours v. sincerely

H. L. Bradfer-Lawrence

A letter from H L Bradfer-Lawrence, a wealthy collector who received
many precious items via Tot and, happily, left most of the relevant
material to the Yorkshire Archaeological Society.

Hither and Thither

IN 1935, Sir Arthur Keith, having attended a meeting of the British Association in Norwich, set out with a friend for "the caves and moors of Yorkshire." On reaching Settle, he inquired about Tot, who had sent him bones for examination. "Failing to find trace of him," Sir Arthur wrote in his autobiography, "we had to drive up the steep road which leads to the high moorland plateau lying immediately to the east of Settle. We were in search of the great Victoria Cave which had been excavated by Boyd Dawkins."

They were driving along at an easy pace "when a hullabaloo broke out behind us. We stopped and looked backwards. A tradesman's van was being driven towards us by a Jehu, and a man on the top of the van was gesticulating wildly. The gesticulating young man turned out to be Tot Lord, who had heard that we had been asking for him. He wanted us to return home and then see his museum and his latest discoveries. That we promised to do some other day. Meanwhile, we asked him and his friend to accompany us to the Victoria Cave."

In 1935, Tot was at another new cave, aptly-named Jubilee Cave after a contemporary Royal occasion, in the hills above Settle. When a mining engineer saw the roof of the cave he took one look and fled. It was a mass of choked boulders that threatened to crush the intrepid seekers after early history. Such a trifle like that did not daunt them. They bought "crash" helmets and began to take away the face of the cave.

In September, 1935, the skeleton of a male and fragments of other skeletons were excavated in this little-known cave in Kings Scar. Sir Arthur Keith, who was on holiday in the district, examined the remains, found under a shelf of rock. Subsequently, to Tot's delight, Sir Arthur sent a report of the skeleton, which he found to be of a man about 5ft 5in in stature, of medium strength of bone a probably over 50 years old. He had the characteristics of the Romano-British folk, his skull being long and narrow.

The teeth of this man, and especially his first molars, were ground down to an extreme degree, showing that his food was rough and gritty. Abscesses had formed at the roots of some of the lower molar teeth. The man suffered from an intense degree of rheumatic changes in all the joints of his backbone – from skull to sacrum. Also his knees were the seats of similar joint changes. Sir Keith identified parts of at least four individuals other than the main burial. These were a girl, a man and two women.

When Tot thought his helpers needed a "quiet week-end" he varied the work by going potholing. One pothole, near Stockdale Farm, Settle, was explored and named Lord's Hole. It was not for the inexperienced, containing unseen dangers. Years later, Ian Plant, who married a granddaughter of Tot, and had a special interest in exploring Lord's Hole, was to write: "Within minutes of a heavy shower, the entrance rift becomes a roaring cataract, thus barring access to the surface if anyone is below. Loose boulders are prominent throughout the upper section and the slightest miscalculation in judging the position of one of these blocks could send the remainder crashing on to the explorer."

Tot discovered what turned out to be a 165ft deep system in 1929 during one of his many outings on the fells and he made a partial descent by rope before returning with a larger party and more equipment. The ladder for the first pitch hung in a fissure barely a foot wide in places but opened out after 15 ft, dropping past several slabs of jammed rock where the explorer swung precariously on the ladder before setting foot on a steep-dipping boulder slope. The main chamber was extremely muddy. From it radiated passages. By this time, exploration was for those who were not unhappy when moving in oozing mud and slime.

Tot was an individualist. Who but he would have taken to a week-long excavation of a site on Malham Moor a marquee and a bed with a brass head? Who but Tot would have installed a stove in the rock shelter known as Sewell's Cave? When working on Sunday, he welcomed his wife as she arrived with the ingredients of a good lunch. It was cooked to a turn and complete with Yorkshire pudding.

Tot was associated with the Craven Pothole Club which in the early 1930s held regular meets at the easier caves and potholes. They hired a bus belonging to the *Pennine* company for the day. The first bus-meet was on August 10, 1930, when Edgar Smith drove a 14-seater Overland bus to Stockdale Farm and Tot introduced the members to Lord's Hole, which Tot had explored earlier in the year. The CPC then moved to South Bank Hole, which Tot had also found, making a second descent of the entrance pitch into a chamber containing many loose boulders.

By the mid-1930s, potholing was thought to need an effective rescue service. An early casualty, in Sunset Hole, in the days when the Yorkshire Ramblers were bottoming many of the major systems, was borne back to the surface using an old door as a stretcher. The door had to be trimmed so much during the rescue it was said to take on the shape of the injured man (who survived the rough treatment).

The Moor & Fell Club, undistinguished with regard to discoveries, unwittingly had a profound influence on the caving scene. On October 13, 1934, nine members held the Club's second meet at Gingling Hole, on Fountains Fell. All reached the final chamber without incident. Then, Reg Weetman dislodged an unstable boulder choke, which crushed his right leg. He sustained a double fracture of the bones and a splint was improvised from a camera tripod.

His colleagues hauled him up the final pitch but Weetman was in such pain he refused to be moved further. Bendle, who had gone for help, found eight members of the Northern Cavern and Fell Club, also Reg Hainsworth, Tot Lord and Godfrey Wilson, the last-named being the art master at Giggleswick School. Reg Weetman's successful rescue was largely a matter of good luck. Fortunately, the NCFC members were available – and still sober when the alarm was raised. The trio of local men were at hand and a stretcher had been available at a local quarry.

Potentially more serious was an accident to Albert Hull, of Bradford, who entered Marble Steps Pot on August 14, 1936, with Frank Butterfield, Harold and Norman Dunnington. He fell when a ladder rung slipped in a feature of the pothole known as the Intestines and received cuts and bruises. Messrs Hainsworth, Lord, Simpson, Thornber and Dr Lovett, of what had become the Central Rescue Organisation (CRO), brought him to the surface in less than five hours.

Tot became one of the first wardens of the Central Rescue Organisation, later known as the Cave Rescue Organisation, the other wardens being Hainsworth, Wilson and Thornber, with Arnold Waterfall making a fifth – and youngest – warden after the 1939-45 war. The most remarkable feature about the Cave Rescue Organisation, as it became, was that it survived the inaugural meeting and was able to help potholers in trouble. This was a major achievement considering the antagonistic personalities of those who were running it.

The committee meetings, with Tot Lord and Messrs Roberts, Simpson and Thornber sitting around the same table, were lively affairs. That the CRO survived is largely due to the political skills of Reg Hainsworth, who maintained good relations with all the cavers of that period. In the late 1940s, the CRO was unorganised, with a Neil Robertson stretcher kept in a cell at the police station. It was said that if you wanted the CRO, you had to send a postcard. The rescue organisation relied on members of the various clubs coming to help and using their own equipment.

Tot was known to go underground but his truly active days were over. He was rising 50, somewhat bulky in appearance, and not really fit enough to be doing this sort of thing. His last recorded rescue bid was when the CRO, using the stretcher and a few mouldy ropes, were summoned to Alum Pot, where potholers, who had gone below in reasonable conditions, were trapped by a sudden rush of water.

Bob Clough was holding one end of a rope. Tot was at the other end of it. He had entered by Long Churn and had not been seen for 20 minutes. Jim Leach went down and found Tot sitting on a ledge, out of the water, which was running like a mill-race. Tot said his old legs had given up. His old nerve had also given up. They got him into the water, pushed him back up the passage and then went looking for the people who were reported trapped. It was, by all account, a bit wild down there. One rescuer was swept off his feet.

Wapping Hall

IN 1937, the old Clubroom being inadequate, Tot organised a "flit" into Wapping Hall, formerly the Primitive Methodist chapel. In acquiring the property he used all his business acumen. The Hall, owned by the Robinson family, had been empty for years when the local Troop of Boy Scouts was formed. Needing a headquarters, they acquired Wapping Hall at a peppercorn rent.

The Scouts painstakingly renovated the building, re-pointing the masonry and fitting glass to shattered windows. When the Scouts had been meeting here for about a year, they were informed that the owners, the Robinson family of Ambleside, had sold the premises to Tot Lord. Out went the Scouts and in went Tot, who ensured that virtually everything, even a stuffed badger, lay behind glass.

Light was provided by a candelabra, one of a set that Tot had acquired from E H Partridge, the aforementioned headmaster of

Giggleswick School, who had decided to replace them in the School chapel with strip-lighting.

Wapping Hall held the objects found at Attermire Cave (1924), Lord's Hole (1929), Sewell's Cave (1930), and Jubilee Cave (1935). On the wall was the coat of arms of the Pig Yard Club, with its pig's head, rope ladder, pick and spade, dragonesque brooch and a human bone with gladiatorial sword. Bones from Jubilee Cave interested Sir Arthur Keith, the eminent anthropologist, who classified the skull and fragments of several skeletons as dating back nearly 3,000 years.

The bones were on view when the British Association met at Settle in September, 1936. Also to be seen was an almost complete skeleton supposed to be of a woman, found near South House Farm, Horton-in-Ribblesdale. In addition, there were iron swords, specimens of bronze brooches, spindle whorls in stone and bone, rubbing stones, flint scrapers, hunting spears and javelins, "all telling interestingly of life in the Dales nearly 2,000 years ago."

Tot's activities came to the attention of some distinguished people, who found the concept of the Pig Yard Club appealing. A president was appointed. He was R M (Maurice) Richards of London, a botanist and specialist in the life of Roman Britain. Sir Arthur Keith advised the Club on anthropology and Arthur Raistrick on other aspects of the work. Dr Arthur Smith Woodward, Dr R G S Hudson and Lady Boyd Dawkins were among those who signed the visitors' book. An unusual sight at Settle about this time was that of Lady Boyd Dawkins and her husband helping in the hayfield rented by Thomas Lord, snr. Tot was obliged to help at haytime. The Boyd Dawkins's, who wished Tot to take them to the caves, contrived to speed up haymaking by lending a hand.

Philip Radley, the Clerk of London and Middlesex Quarterly Meeting of the Quakers, spent part of a summer holiday in the Yorkshire Dales in the company of his mother and son Patrick. They "archaeologised, geologised and fraternised." Philip, writing in *The Friend* of September 2, 1938, described the Pig Yard Club he had visited as "a working men's geological and archaeological society."

An Eye for a Bargain

IN THE DAYS when he was stripping-down old cars, Tot had a cheerful helper in Tom Dugdale. In later life, the friendship continued spasmodically – more precisely, when Tot wanted a lift anywhere, for Tom had the opportunity of using his father's motor wagon. Tot, anxious to attend a sale at Kilnsey, asked Tom if he was attending. He said "No" but was not averse to driving him there. At the sale, Tot did not buy a single object. The two clambered into the wagon for the return. A little way down the road, the cylinder head gasket blew and the water drained from the radiator.

Tot remarked that John Bell, the driver of a quarry lorry who lived on the Shambles at Settle, was still at the pub before returning home. He agreed to tow the two men and their defective motor vehicle back to town "for a consideration" – namely, one pint, which was promptly purchased for him. He said there was a steam roller nearby with a chain on it. He would borrow the chain and return it next morning. The massive chain was fixed to the front axle. The next stop was outside the *Devonshire* at Cracoe, where Mr Bell thought he could do with another consideration.

He was by this time at the "merry" stage, even more so when – a mile or so further along the road – he stopped at the *Angel* at Hetton and requested yet another pint. The rest of the journey to Settle, via Gargrave, was a nightmare, with a worried Tot repeatedly applying the brakes, without effect and with Mr Bell turning repeatedly in the lorry to grin or laugh at them.

At Settle, Bell stopped at Halsteads. Tom said his father's motor wagon would have to be left at Ellis's garage, just across the road. A strong smell came from the red-hot brakes. The axle was bent forward. The front tyres had no tread left on them. Father was not very pleased to receive a repair bill for £50, which in 1931 was an appreciable sum of money.

In 1938, Geoffrey Dawson, Editor of *The Times*, who lived at Langcliffe Hall and showed great interest in Tot's activities, modified the approaches to the Hall, which made an iron gate redundant. Naturally, Tot showed interest in it and eventually it was serving its original purpose at the home of the Simpsons at Gargrave. When, after the war, the contents of Lowther Castle, the vast family home of Lord Lonsdale near Penrith came up for sale, prior to the demolition of all but the façade, Tot was among those present.

He attended with his friends the Simpsons of Gargrave and also had the company of his son, Thomas, shortened to Tom. They wandered through vast suites, each with its distinctive colour. They noticed that the Yellow Earl's toilet had a velvet-lined seat. Tom set his heart on buying (for scrap) the big brass staircase but the scrap price did not apply. There were people present who wanted to preserve it as a masterpiece in another setting.

Tot, the businessman, bought the *White Horse* at Settle, closed it down and had the licence transferred (for a consideration) to the *Ashfield*, which had been a temperance hotel. Tot bought stately homes, stripping lead from their roofs and anything else that was saleable, leaving them as shells. This happened to Hellifield Peel, the second oldest inhabited house in Craven (after Skipton Castle).

The peel, or pele, had at its core one of those fortified towers built to withstand a siege during the uneasy period of Scottish raids. When Sir William Nicholson died in 1944, the Peel was a splendid place. I remember visiting it as a reporter on the staff of the *Craven Herald* and being impressed by this venerable building, rising above well-manicured gardens. The Hellifield Peel estate was requisitioned as a prisoner of war camp. The voices of Italians, then Germans, echoed in its spacious rooms.

Tot came into the story after the estate had been sold by Dorothy, last of the Hammerton family, to Lunds of Otley, who were wood merchants keen to harvest a crop of splendid trees on a 360-acre estate on the rich earth of mid-Craven. Others took away the oak floors. Tot asked a friend to cart some material from Hellifield and when the friend arrived he saw Tot taking off the heavy interior doors. He had already sold the roof lead for a good price.

The contents of Ingmire Hall, at Sedbergh, were auctioned over two days, the hall itself being sold on the third day. The appointed time was 3-00. Tot, who never drove a vehicle, once again asked a friend to take him there. At the time the hall was to be sold, Tot was nowhere to be seen. Eventually this fine property was knocked down for £3,000. A buzz went round that Lord Somebody had bought it. Tot's friend waited for him to appear and eventually returned to Settle without him.

The next time he was seen, he was emerging from the outfitters' shop of John Moore about 10-00 on Thursday morning. He confessed to having bought Ingmire Hall. He had to sign up for it and at the same time pay a 10% deposit, which was £300. He hadn't got the money to lodge in the bank before his cheque went through. Tot, having just borrowed £50 from John Moore, was on his way to see Mr Wallace, the jeweller, for another loan. Eventually he got his £300 and put it in the bank. His first plan was to strip the lead off the roof, sell it and recover the purchase price on the hall. He was not allowed to do this until he had made full payment. Tot was thus in a bit of a plight. One morning, when his friend went to work, he heard a buzz going round Settle that Ingmire Hall had gone up in smoke.

The story that Tot was going to claim the insurance was hardly true because the property did not actually belong to him. There was talk of arson, but Tot had been no where near when whoever it was poured petrol all over the place. Posters that went up in Settle offered £50 reward for anyone giving information leading to the arrest and conviction of the arsonist. For a few days, detectives swarmed in the town. They never did find out who applied the match to Ingmire Hall.

Another property that interested Tot was a big old hall in the East Riding. It was truly large, being the sort of place where one might wander about for hours without exhausting the rooms. The owner, a member of a notable local family, had slowly withdrawn into a corner of the vast building. Here she lived, simply, until there was nothing to do but sell the property. When she sold it to Tot, she knew that he intended to demolish it.

As soon as Tot had paid for the hall, she persuaded the local council to apply for a preservation order. Tot was effectively barred from doing anything with the building that would give him a quick return. He tried to get the order rescinded. He sold off the substantial vegetable gardens to a farmer who promptly converted it into a field. Tot had some valuable fishing rights. When, eventually, the preservation order was removed, the price of lead had gone down so much it was not worth the cost of removing it. The hall, sold for a modest sum, was restored, with grants, and became a school. Tot still had the lucrative fishing rights.

A crucial friendship for Tot was with Bradfer-Lawrence, of Ripon, who collected rare and precious objects of Yorkshire interest. Tot provided Bradfer-Lawrence with old documents he came across at various sales knowing that payment would be prompt and generous. One day, Tot persuaded a young friend to drive him to Stratford-on-Avon with a parcel wrapped in old newspaper. At Stratford, he inquired the way to the home of J B Priestley. The great man had not met Tot before. "Nay" said Tot, "I thought you might like to see this." He parted the newspaper wrapping to reveal an illuminated medieval book he had borrowed from Bradfer-Lawrence, who referred to his Settle friend as "Master Tot."

Happily, the material that Tot funnelled through Bradfer-Lawrence would be left to the archive of the Yorkshire Archaeological Society. Tot, who was an impulsive man, could be generous. He made a gift of volumes to the Library of the British Speleological Association at Buxton. The hon. secretary wrote in August, 1936: "I assure you that we do appreciate your great interest and kindness." Already the proverbial war clouds were gathering. Maurice Richards, writing to Tot from 47, Whitehall, London, in October, 1938, was happy with Appeasement. "We may all be thankful that you have not been called upon to be anything more than Chief Air Raid Warden or that I have not been called up by the War Office, or that any of us are not wondering when our term for the devil of a long trip will come," he wrote. "It is far better to have peace at a price than war, the outcome of which would have meant death for many of us and ruin for the rest of us."

In 1945, Albert Mitchell, now an Army major, serving in South East Asia Command, acknowledged a letter sent to him through an Air Letter, "unit censored," addressed simply to Mr Tot Lord, P.Y.C Museum, Settle, Yorks, England. Albert began with great cordiality: "My Dear Tot." He lamented the loss of a mutual friend, "our fellow archaeologist, Tommy Briggs." Albert could say little about the Asian geology. It was "the lias type of stuff we met around Newcastle. There's plenty of that here but most of the old stuff is well buried. There are few faults in the Yorkshire sense of the word but most of the strata dips. Limestone I have not seen since I left England."

He was more enthusiastic about the Brahmaputra, "the biggest glacial valley I've seen, now fed in winter from the melting snows and in summer by torrential rain. And when it rains here, it puts any Yorkshire potholing weather in the shade." Albert ended his letter: "My regards to your wife and please do tell her that I'm looking forward to you and I (after a day in the hills) sitting down to one of her special dishes."

Alum Pot

Life at Town Head

IN 1948, Tot and his family moved to Town Head, a large Victorian house with a park-like setting. This imposing building, which had been the residence of Dr Edgar and his family, was originally known as Town End. It was the third substantial house to occupy the site. When the original was built, it stood at the Castleberg bar gate to a packhorse track leading diagonally up the hillside to "Malham Mere." This house was enlarged in 1770 and reconstructed about 1870.

A special architectural feature remaining throughout was a vaulted cellar, not unlike a Norman crypt, the outer walls of which were over 6 ft thick. Tot packed it with cases of stuffed birds and animals until they had an appeal for someone who gained entry through a tunnel under the Langcliffe road and surreptitiously removed them.

Into Town Head, which now was partly lagged by the mould of dry rot, bringing the property into a speculator's price range, moved Tot, his family and an archaeological collection that included the Victoria and Attermire Cave collections and no less than 20,000 documents of historic interest. Tot had great plans and greater hopes for Town Head. Before long, there were several partly-completed jobs.

Tot preferred the open air to the dusty recesses of a large house. When members of the Craven Pothole Club intermittently put in much hard work at a point in the dry valley about 150 yards below Malham Tarn Sinks, and hoped to enter a large system, Tot and some explosives were summoned to help the explorers on their way. He arrived at the dig, grunting and grumbling about his sciatica. He moved stiffly into the hole, lit the fuse, then shot out like a spring rabbit, in case there was any air in the packing.

Not all his plans for Town Head were to be realised. He knocked down walls to make some big rooms downstairs and began to establish a museum. But, being Tot, his restless mind would not allow him to finish it. He took up the rotten floorboards of the ground floor and concreted it. Tot intended - one day, soon, perhaps - to establish a rock garden and also to open the grounds to those members of the public who would appreciate "a quiet secluded spot where they can sit in the sunshine and enjoy the splendid panorama of the Craven countryside." He had many visitors. The Universities of Leeds and Manchester looked upon him as a fairy godmother and did much to encourage him.

To walk up the short drive to the house from the top of Constitution Hill was to enter an area that, with its dense shrubbery, its old palm tree, and the big house with glass-and-iron verandah, might almost have been a film set for a story penned by Somerset Maugham. Sound effects included the cackling of guinea fowl. Butterflies by the score occupied the sunlit days in visiting the many buddleias.

Beneath the verandah reposed Tot, using a wicker chair, which stood by a table and – the skull of an elephant. Just inside the hall, which was adorned by Minton tiles, a man-trap hung from a wall. If Tot was no where to be seen, it was almost certain that his old collie was tied up by the door, the rope being just long enough to bring the threshold of the door within snapping distance.

Apart from family possessions, this house contained bleached skulls and bones of ancient beasts, Roman coins, early pottery, fossils, precious scripts, arrowheads, tracts and books and posters of long ago. If Tot was not otherwise engaged, he would cordially invite a caller to a tour of his museum. Otherwise, he would dash off to the Nuvic Cinema, where he had his own special end seat.

One who was allowed to enter saw that the sides of a flight of stairs that curved out of sight on its way to an upper storey held stacks of back numbers of *Country Life*. Upstairs, the family home was one gigantic flat from which it was possible to walk on the level and gain the high road to Langcliffe through a doorway in the wall.

The museum was in a large ground floor room on the left. After the ritualistic unlocking of the door there was a glorious insight into the past, neatly arranged in glass-sided display cases which were not locked in the conventional sense but secured by screws that had to be removed when entry was necessary and a heavy glass lid must be removed. Tot acquired glass from many sources. In some cases, he purchased old mirrors and scraped them clean with razor blades, leaving large pieces of high quality plate glass.

The museum had a Victorian character. Items were arranged neatly. Here was the skull of a great cave bear and there an exquisite reverse barbed harpoon head fashioned from antler. One item, from the discoveries when Victoria Cave had been excavated, was labelled Bone of Contention because the experts had not been able to decide if it was human or animal.

Finely-worked dragonesque brooches, from the latest period of cave occupation, contrasted with the pathetically few bones – the remains of so-called Ingleborough Woman, found among the clints near South House, North Ribblesdale, when these were being systematically removed by Dick Preston of Ingleton, to provide weathered limestone for suburban gardens. The exhibit of the female bones included an axe, though in truth this was found at least 600 ft from where the woman had been laid to rest.

A newspaper correspondent described Town Head, in the days of Tot, as "a polyglot temple dedicated to the past." The "old house" was "buried in an untamed tree-girt garden at the top of a steep, narrow lane running behind the Shambles in Settle market-place" being "more than a relic of the past itself." Over this "unique private museum," Tot Lord, greengrocer by trade, potholer and archaeologist by choice, presided with pride.

The writer, somewhat confused by the contents of the temple, mentioned that the bony remains included the skull of a man of 1,000 BC. "That the Celtic gentleman was probably a cannibal seems more than likely, for in Jubilee Cave, where his remains were found, were other human bones which analysis showed to have been cooked, and which had clearly not got into niches in the rock of their own accord. Roman relics found in Attirmire [sic] testify to the stout defence put up by the 'Maquis' of the Roman invasion period – the Brigantes who had their stronghold in the Settle area. From the caves to which they retreated, they raided the invading forces, carrying loot back to the caves where for hundreds of years it lay hidden." Perhaps.

Arthur Raistrick, who had inspired Tot and his friends to go cave-hunting, benefited largely from the objects found, and it is likely that Tot regarded it as a reciprocal arrangement, nurturing the hope that Raistrick would write up their work under both names. Raistrick (November, 1949) indicated that "Richmond and I are still working on the drawings of your bronzes, and they are proving a most interesting lot, probably one of the finest collections in the North of England. They have set no end of problems and are giving us a new light on the Brigantes. You have done a magnificent work there, Tot, and I hope it will be possible to make your work known. You have done more than many professionals could. What we begin to know of the real Brigantian culture we owe to you." Arthur wished him good luck "with your new place."

Having been showed through the new museum, Raistrick wrote (April, 1950) to express his pleasure at the work Tot had done. "I never imagined you could make such a fine museum of the ground floor of the house. When I saw it with you, and heard your plans, I could see a good place coming out of it, but certainly nothing so brilliant as the arrangement you have made. It is a monument to your vision, patience and magnificent work."

Tot had found the fragment of an Anglo-Danish cross shaft at Long Preston and important Beaker fragments on Malham Moor. Arthur's letter alluded to them and concluded: "I will get over to Settle some Monday soon, and will draw the cross, the Long Preston implements, etc, and will get them published almost at once so that you can have a stock of reprints for the Museum. I have gone on fairly steadily with the description of the other stuff and when you get set out can make a really good short description of the show and help with some diagrams, etc. I arranged recently to get some of your stuff published and can reserve a good deal of that space for your new and most important find. Will talk things over when I come along."

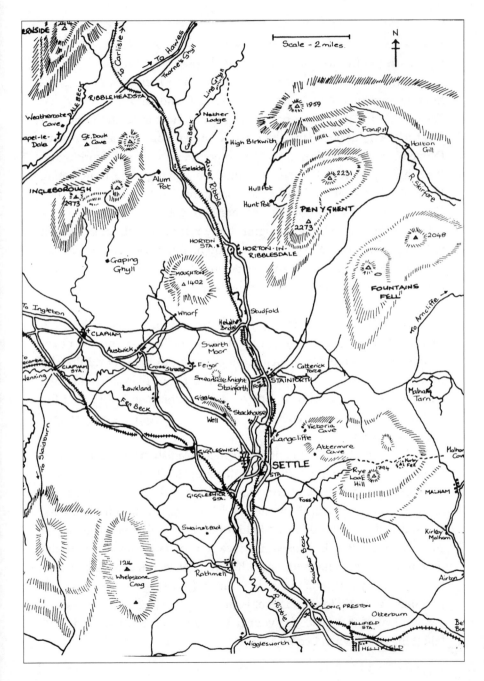

In the Field

A MONG THE surplus equipment sold off cheaply at the end of the 1939-45 war were mine-detectors. Tot early saw the possibility of using these in field archaeology. He used a detector at Attermire Camp and Roman coins were found.

In September, 1952, Tot and some of his friends were encamped near "a peculiar mound" in Low Henside pasture, above Cowside Farm, which in turn is near Langcliffe. The friends were E Douglas, the son of E J W Douglas, clerk to the Settle District Education Sub-Committee, Alf Sewell, and Robert Breaks. A *Craven Herald* reporter who visited the camp saw two tents with the Union Jack flying above one of them. "The party moved into camp with pick-axes, spades, shovels and a wheelbarrow…and already they have excavated a considerable area. It is their intention to cut two trenches through the mound – one from north to south and the other at right angles – and this, they think, will lay bare some primary or secondary interment."

Tot was quoted as saying that the mound was probably erected for the burial of the chieftain of some ancient race, who will probably lie in the centre. "The tumuli, however, has been worn by the weather for at least 2,000 years and the centre to-day may not be the centre of the time when Craven was peopled by Celts and Ancient Britons."

On May 3, 1940, when Norman Thornber recovered a lamb from a pothole near Stockdale Farm, Tot was holding the lifeline. For this rescue, they were awarded merit certificates by the RSPCA. A wartime mystery concerned the discovery of an abandoned tent at Alum Pot, above Selside, on July 10, 1943. A packet of food was located at the entrance to Long Churn Cave, part of the same system. The police called out the CRO and Tot was among the party who searched the caves, also Diccan Pot. Reg Hainsworth and Norman Thornber descended Alum Pot but no one was found.

After the War

IN 1949, the 700th anniversary of the granting of a market charter by Henry Percy was celebrated at Settle and Tot, as one of the councillors, was transformed. His tweedy clothes gave way to a smart dark suit. His ruddy complexion took on an extra brightness as he played his part in this momentous event.

When he borrowed the Settle market charter from Bradfer-Lawrence, there were some who wondered how the wealthy collector had acquired it in the first place. Bradfer-Lawrence, ever-grateful for Tot's help as a collector of special bygones, occasionally came to his assistance when, for the moment, he was strapped for cash.

In the 1950s, Tot had become, in the words of a local journalist, "an amusing and likeable personality who has figured in several BBC broadcasts on North Country topics. Mr Lord may be termed the guardian of North Ribblesdale's past. He is always on the lookout for interesting things, old and new. "Not only did he carry to his museum the village stocks, which were in danger of being destroyed; he went to the trouble of saving a special AA road sign made in June 1927 to direct traffic to Giggleswick for the total eclipse of the sun. Giggleswick was in the direct line of totality; in fact the Astronomer Royal made his observations at Giggleswick School. "That road sign will be valuable some day."

His long-time friendship with Arthur Simpson, of Gargrave, brought many rewards, not least the distinction of having his portrait painted by Arnold Mason, RA, of Chaney Walk, London, who occasionally visited the Simpson. It was Mason, an imposing figure, being tall, aristocratic, with a spade-type beard, who painted a portrait of E H Partridge which hangs in the School hall. When it was Tot's turn to be painted, he was pictured glancing down at the jaw bone of an extinct species of rhinoceros from the Pig Yard collection.

In his later years, Tot explored the Hambleton Hills, bringing back to Town Head, in small cloth bags, a host of flints. Tot was never taught how to drive a car and was content to be seen in a distinguished vehicle, such as Arthur Simpson's 1952 Bentley. "He sat in it like Lord Muck." It was Arthur who bought him a Land Rover with a long wheelbase, registered number 721 BWR.

Young Donnie, one of several voluntary chauffeurs, recalls that the sandwiches packed for the mid-day snack were invariably salmon and cucumber, though the first stop was at a café in Thirsk for a meat pie and tea in a pint pot. The Pig Yard Club crest, painted on the doors, was useful on the day when Miss Worsley, of Hovingham, married the Duke of Kent and roads in the Helmsley district were congested. Seeing the crest, a policeman waved Tot's party through a temporary road block.

John and Margaret Bielby, farmers on the Hambleton Hills, provided a home-from-home for the flint seekers from Settle. On Sundays, they invited the visitors to share an evening meal – a real North Country meal, with Yorkshire pudding served at the start as a separate, gravy-covered dish. Each Christmas, Tot would go the rounds of farmer friends in the area, handing out packets of biscuits – Chocolate Vienna – as a mark of appreciation.

Back at Settle, the Land Rover was parked in garage formed with walls of bales of straw and a roof consisting of sheets of corrugated zinc. The Land Rover was eventually purchased to carry members of a Scottish school's canoe club and their canoes. At the request of Tot, the Pig Yard Club crest was removed from the doors and the space occupied by one for the canoe club.

Luck was certainly on Tot's side. He acquired the Giggleswick School share of the Victoria Cave finds. Another fine haul was most of the contents of the museum established by the Settle Naturalist Society when the museum was closed in the 1950s, the building in which it was housed being proclaimed unsafe. When the Farrers left Ingleborough Hall, Tot was given an opportunity to look through the attics and keep anything of interest. One item, a piece of stone with runic instruction, turned up in his Victoria Cave collection, though in fact it was a copy of a stone found by one of the Farrers, a notable archaeologist, during excavations in the Northern Isles.

Outings with Mr Partridge

SOCIAL distinctions counted for nothing when Tot met E H Partridge by the Ribble on winter evenings when a flight of duck was expected. Partridge, writing about his sporting life in the Ribble Valley at the "edge o' dark," as local people call dusk, was to recall in particular the brightness of Tot's face – "a red face which in the fading light had the dull glow of old baked brick."

One evening, when Partridge was with Tot and his son, crouching near the river, waiting for the ducks to flight, "the full humour of the situation dawned on me. We were a representative company – a parent who was also an Old Boy, a Day Boy and the Headmaster. And if the pupil was playing truant from preparation, the Headmaster was pretty certainly poaching. And I laughed till I could hardly shoot as I thought of the long spoon a man needs who would sup with the devil. But we got nine mallard, two wigeon and a teal."

There was a time when Tot fished – with a gun. Tot suddenly swung the firearm and discharged a barrel at the astonished Head's legs as he waded in the shallows, his mind intent on birds. "The water was cut to foam behind me, and as I turned to ask him with some wealth of anathema what the game was, I was cut short by a peremptory 'Look sharp! There's your ruddy breakfast'." Partridge turned to see a fine grayling, of about $1^1/_2$lb, floating belly upwards. Tot, in reply to the other man's wonderment that he should have fired directly at him, said: "You're wearing gum-boots, aren't you?"

The Sunset Days

IN THE 1960s, Harold Walker, a regular companion of Tot in the open air, took him at Tot's request to a point near Malham Cove where he was instructed to park the car. They walked across the clints. Tot went unerringly to a place where soil and sticks lay in a gryke. He pulled away this soft material to expose a quern. Tot told Harold he had found and hidden that quern in 1925.

Tot's collection of local documents was outstanding. When he heard that a young couple had bought a particular old house, Tot produced "something that might interest you." It was the original deed, in which Henry Whittam, gentleman of Knaresborough, bought Orchard Garth...

Tot and his old friend Tom Dugdale met in Chapel Street. Tot said he was going to his solicitors' office. He had bought Cleatop and had to pay for it by Thursday. He hadn't the money to meet the bill. Tot raised cash quickly by selling some of the land to local farmers. He arranged to clear-fell the wood and subsequently persuaded a forestry organisation to replant it in exchange for the land. Tot shrewdly retained the shooting rights.

Tot's partiality for incinerating cigarettes by the yard possibly shortened his life. He died on October 21, 1965, aged sixty-six. The funeral took place in the afternoon of October 25, when at a service held in Settle Parish Church the hymns sung were "Guide me, O Thou great Jehovah" and "Mine eyes have seen the coming of the Lord." Cremation took place at Skipton. Under the terms of his will, Tot's ashes were scattered on Attermire Scar.

Yet, like John Brown, his soul goes marching on. It is said that when, within a short time of Tot's death, Town Head was demolished, the driver of a JCB felt his scalp prickling as he sensed a ghostly presence. Tot Lord made a lasting mark on local archaeology. Sir Arthur Keith, inscribing to Tot a copy of his autobiography, published in 1950, wrote: "You have been a great pioneer in what you have done for the 'pre-histories' of Settle. We are all your debtors."

To Partridge, the company of Tot had always been invigorating. He wrote: "To spend an hour in Tot's company is to slip back to the zest and inconsequent humour of childhood applied to the affairs of a grown-up, workaday world."

Quick comments from friends and associates...

If you knew Tot, you'll never forget him.
Personality oozed from him.
He was ruddy-faced. Brilliantly ruddy-faced.
He had character.
He managed to do without work.
Tot never seemed to have any money when he went about with us.
Tot was wheeling and dealing in all sorts of things.
He had some amazing friendships. Tot liked being with the gentry.
Tot loved his Aga cooker.
He was a bit of a romancer.

Acknowledgements

Great help was given by Tom Lord (grandson of Tot), by Chrissie and Margaret Lord (his daughter and granddaughter), Jim Lord (brother-in-law) and other members of the family. Also Margaret Breaks, Stephen A Craven, Tom Dugdale, Leonard Dutton, Lloyd Fletcher, Alan King, Jim Leach, Jack Myers, Jim Nelson, Mrs Arthur Simpson, Edgar Smith and Harold Walker.

Drawings by E. Jeffrey and Godfrey Wilson.

Front cover portrait by Arnold Mason, R.A.
Back cover photograph by the author.

A Cave Diver